From Fail to Win!
Learning from Bad Ideas

MILITARY and
GOVERNMENT TECHNOLOGY

Ian Graham

www.raintreepublishers.co.uk
Visit our website to find out more information about Raintree books.

To order:
☎ Phone 0845 6044371
▤ Fax +44 (0) 1865 312263
▣ Email myorders@raintreepublishers.co.uk

Customers from outside the UK please telephone +44 1865 312262

Raintree is an imprint of Capstone Global Library Limited, a company incorporated in England and Wales having its registered office at 7 Pilgrim Street, London, EC4V 6LB – Registered company number: 6695582

Text © Capstone Global Library Limited 2011
First published in hardback in 2011
The moral rights of the proprietor have been asserted.

Edited by Andrew Farrow and
   Vaarunika Dharmapala
Designed by Richard Parker
Original illustrations © Capstone Global
   Library Ltd 2011
Illustrated by Jeff Edwards
Picture research by Mica Brancic
Originated by Capstone Global Library Ltd
Printed and bound in China by South China
   Printing Company Ltd

ISBN 978 1 406 21764 3 (hardback)
14 13 12 11 10
10 9 8 7 6 5 4 3 2 1

British Library Cataloguing in Publication Data
Graham, Ian.
From fail to win : learning from bad ideas.
Military and government technology.
623-dc22
A full catalogue record for this book is available from the British Library.

Acknowledgements
We would like to thank the following for permission to reproduce photographs: Alamy pp. **10** (© www.white-windmill.co.uk), **21** (© Interfoto), **35** (© Rick & Nora Bowers); Corbis pp. **5** (© Bettmann), **8** (© Liam Davis), **19, 20** (© Aero Graphics, Inc.), **27** (© Museum of Flight/Gordon S. Williams), **28** (© Smithsonian Institution), **30** (© Reuters/TRW, Inc.), **32** (© Bettmann), **45** (Reuters/© Fabrizio Bensch), **47** (© Bettmann), **48** (© Bettmann), **49** (© Reuters); Courtesy of Jasper Yellowhead Museum & Archives, PA7-2, Fred Brewster fonds p. **17**; Getty Images pp. **7** (Science & Society Picture Library/Science Museum), **38** (Stone/Erik Simonsen), **42** (De Agostini Picture Library), **43** (National Geographic/Joseph E. Barrett), **44** (National Geographic/Hervey Garret Smith), **46** (Hulton Archive/Pictorial Parade); Imperial War Museum Film Frames Collection p. **39**; Mondolithic Studios Inc. p. **15** (Kenn Brown); Museum of Artillery, Engineers and Signal Corps, St Petersburg p. **36** (Yuri Pasholok); Rex Features p. **22** (Sipa Press); Wikipedia p. **11**.

Cover photograph of a tail section of a navy blimp with the Stokes cloud from Operation Plumbbob in the background, Clark County, Nevada, USA, reproduced with permission of Corbis (Science Faction/© National Nuclear Security Administration).

We would like to thank Mark Adamic for his invaluable help in the preparation of this book.

Every effort has been made to contact copyright holders of material reproduced in this book. Any omissions will be rectified in subsequent printings if notice is given to the publisher.

Contents

Any words appearing in the text in bold, **like this**,
are explained in the glossary

Lessons learned

Scientists, engineers, and inventors are always thinking up new vehicles and machines. Many of their ideas are successful, but others fail. Sometimes valuable lessons are learned from the failures.

Lots of new ideas and inventions are tried during wars in an attempt to give military forces a technological advantage over their enemies. Governments are also keen to use the latest inventions and clever ideas to collect information about enemies, and possible future enemies, by spying on them. Tanks, fighter planes, spy-planes, and bombers were developed during World War I (1914–1918). Rocket-propelled missiles, pilotless aircraft, jet fighters, rocket-powered fighter planes, atomic bombs, **radar**, and electronic computers were developed during World War II (1939–1945). Spy satellites were developed during the Cold War (see panel). However, other inventions and ideas were not as successful as these.

The Cold War

The Cold War was a time of tension and conflict between the **USSR** and the United States. It lasted from 1945 until 1991, when the USSR collapsed. The Cold War triggered a nuclear arms race, the Space Race, and technological competition between the two states.

Why inventions fail

There are many reasons why new ideas fail. Some of them don't work well enough to be worthwhile. Others are too expensive to develop. Some inventions and ideas are ahead of their time. The famous Italian artist, scientist, engineer, and inventor Leonardo da Vinci (1452–1519) produced dozens of great ideas. He thought of the parachute, bicycle, machine-gun, helicopter, diving suit, and all

Leonardo da Vinci drew this design for a helicopter-like vehicle in the late 15th century, but it was not built in da Vinci's time. The modern helicopter was invented more than 400 years later, in the early 20th century.

sorts of other wonderful machines. However, many of them could not be built successfully for hundreds of years, because the materials needed to make them or the engines needed to drive them did not exist in da Vinci's time.

From fail to win

If an invention fails, it may not disappear forever. As time goes on, new advances in science and technology may make it worthwhile to look at old ideas again. For example, planes without tails, called flying wings, were not a success when they were built in the 1940s. Advances in materials and computers meant that the idea was worth looking at again in the 1980s. The result this time was a very successful military aircraft, the Northrop B-2 Spirit bomber. So, failures can become winners.

As we count down from 13 to 1 in this book, the failures become more serious and the lessons learned are more useful. Comparing one failure with another is not an exact science, so the order in which the projects are ranked is a matter of opinion. How would you rank them?

The *Turtle*   No.13

In 1776, Britain and the United States were at war. British warships were anchored in New York harbour. In an attempt to free the harbour, American forces used a new weapon, a submarine.

On the night of 6 September 1776, British soldiers on the shore of New York harbour spotted something in the water near a British warship, HMS *Eagle*. The object in the water turned out to be a submarine called the *Turtle*. It wasn't the first submarine ever built, but it was the first to attack a ship.

The wooden egg

On the night of the attack, the pilot of the *Turtle* was Continental Sergeant Ezra Lee. He climbed down inside the *Turtle* and the hatch was sealed shut. Lee could see out through six small windows in the brass **conning tower** at the top. The conning tower stood just 20 centimetres (8 inches) above the water. He looked at his compass to see in which direction he had to go to reach HMS *Eagle*. He could see the compass at night because its dial was marked with foxfire, a fungus that glows in the dark.

Lee submerged the *Turtle* just below the surface by opening a valve to let water flow into a **ballast tank**. As the *Turtle* took in water, it grew heavier and sank lower in the water. He moved the submarine by turning two propellers by hand. One, on top, made the *Turtle* move up or down in the water. The other moved it forwards or backwards. A rudder at the back could be turned to one side or the other to steer the *Turtle*.

FAIL!

This is a modern copy of the *Turtle*. It was an egg-shaped craft made of oak and waterproofed with tar. The original was built by David Bushnell in 1776.

The first submarine

Englishman William Bourne described a diving craft in 1578, but did not build it. The Dutchman Cornelis Drebbel built the first submarine in the 1620s. It was demonstrated in the River Thames in London. It was probably a wooden boat-shaped craft covered with leather and propelled by oars.

Attacking the *Eagle*

Ezra Lee watched his compass to make sure he kept heading in the right direction. When he reached HMS *Eagle*, he tried to attach a 68-kilogram (150-pound) explosive charge to its hull using a screw. The plan was to then start a clockwork **fuse**, which would give Lee enough time to move away to a safe distance before the charge exploded. However, he was unable to attach the charge to the *Eagle's* hull. He tried several times, but he had to give up because he was running out of air. As he returned to land, he released the charge into the water. When it exploded with a huge bang, it sent a fountain of water flying high up into the air.

The *Turtle* had no air supply. Tests on modern copies, such as this one, show that the air in it lasted for about 45 minutes before the pilot would have to surface and take in fresh air.

New *Turtles*

Replicas (modern copies) of the *Turtle* have been built and tested. The tests showed that the *Turtle* worked, but it was difficult and dangerous to operate. It could easily dive too deep or crash into things. It was also hard work for the pilot, who had to turn the propellers, turn the rudder, and operate water pumps, all by hand. Piloting the *Turtle* took strength, stamina, and courage.

What was learned?

Although the *Turtle*'s attack on HMS *Eagle* failed, the explosion it set off forced the British to move 200 of their ships to anchor further away. The *Turtle* showed everyone that a submarine could be a useful weapon for attacking ships. It inspired later inventors and engineers to build bigger, better, more powerful, and more deadly submarines.

The *Hunley*

Submarines were used by both sides during the American Civil War (1861–1865). The **Confederate** submarine CSS *Hunley* was the first submarine to attack a ship successfully during a war. On 17 February 1864 it rammed a harpoon into the hull of the USS *Housatonic*, a **Union** warship anchored off Charleston, South Carolina. Then it backed away, leaving behind the harpoon and an explosive charge attached to it. The charge exploded and sank the *Housatonic*. Unfortunately, the *Hunley* also sank immediately after the attack.

Acoustic mirrors

During World War I (1914–1918), British scientists invented a way to hear enemy aircraft coming before they were close enough to be seen. This gave anti-aircraft gunners early warning of bombing raids.

Researchers built concrete dishes called **acoustic mirrors**. They reflected sound in the same way that glass mirrors reflect light. Their curved shape reflected sound to a point in front of the mirror. A cone placed there collected the sound and sent it along rubber tubes to earpieces worn by a listener. Later, a microphone replaced the cone. The cone or microphone was moved about in front of the dish until the sound was loudest. This showed which direction aircraft were coming from.

Acoustic mirrors were built on the north-east and south-east coasts of England. Most of them were dishes up to about 5 metres (16 feet) across, but the biggest was a curved wall that was 61 metres (200 feet) long at Dungeness in Kent, on the south-east coast.

War tuba

In the 1920s and 1930s, several countries tried using giant horns, called acoustic locators, to hear enemy planes approaching and locate enemy **artillery**. One of these early devices was called the Japanese war tuba, because it looked like a musical instrument.

This is one of the dish-shaped acoustic mirrors built on the coast of Kent to detect the sound of approaching enemy aircraft.

Early warning

Experiments with the 61-metre (200-foot) wall showed it was possible to hear a plane 40 kilometres (25 miles) away – four times further than with unaided ears. The acoustic mirrors seemed to be a great success. However, by the outbreak of World War II in 1939, bombers could fly nearly three times faster than in World War I, so the mirrors no longer gave enough warning. The development of **radar** in the 1940s finally made acoustic mirrors **obsolete**. Radar could detect aircraft nearly five times further away than the mirrors.

These strange acoustic devices were known as "war tubas" (see panel on page 10).

Hearing noises

Sound is still used to locate enemy attacks today, but in a different way. Microphones on tall masts listen for the bang of an artillery gun or **mortar** launcher being fired. The sounds picked up by the microphones are analysed by computer. The location of the firing position appears on a map on the computer's screen almost instantly. The enemy position can then be attacked quickly, before the enemy has time to move the firing position.

What was learned?

The acoustic mirrors worked, but by the time they were needed they had been overtaken by new technology – faster aircraft. However, they were valuable in another way. The idea of building a chain of early warning stations around the coast was taken up by the new radar systems that replaced the mirrors during World War II.

Balloon bombs

In 1944, Japan attacked the United States with flying bombs. These flying bombs weren't aircraft, rockets, or guided missiles. They were balloons!

Each balloon was 10 metres (33 feet) across. They were made of mulberry paper, glued together with potato flour paste and filled with **hydrogen** gas, which is lighter than air. More than 9,000 of these balloons were launched into the upper **atmosphere**. There, they were blown eastwards across the Pacific Ocean by a fast wind called the jet stream (see panel).

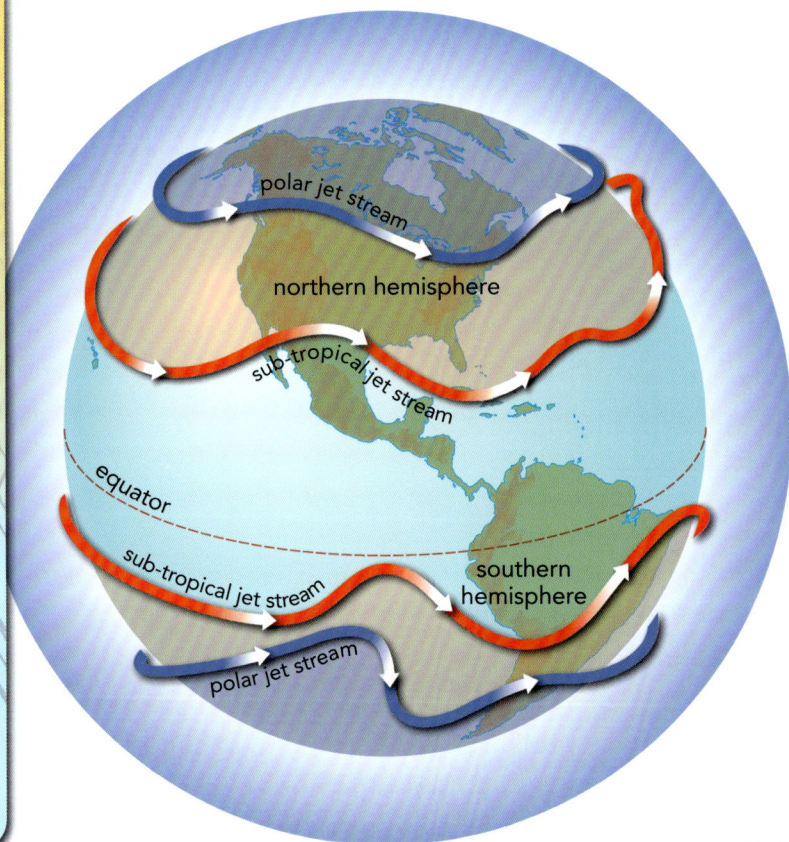

The jet stream

In the 1920s, a Japanese weather scientist called Wasaburo Ooishi discovered a fast wind blowing across Japan towards the east all year round. He published his findings. However, he published his work in a language called Esperanto, which few people understood. As a result, his work was almost entirely unknown outside Japan. Ooishi had discovered one of the "jet streams" – rivers of high-speed wind that blow around the world.

Jet streams are fast winds that blow where air masses of different temperatures meet. They blow around the world about 11 kilometres (7 miles) above the ground.

polar jet stream

northern hemisphere

sub-tropical jet stream

equator

sub-tropical jet stream

southern hemisphere

polar jet stream

Rise and fall

Hydrogen balloons rise in the warmth of the day and sink lower when they cool down at night. It was important to keep the balloon bombs inside the jet stream, so their height had to be controlled. When the balloons flew higher than 11,600 metres (38,000 feet), they automatically let out some hydrogen to bring them down again. When they sank below 9,000 metres (29,500 feet), they dropped bags of sand to make them rise again. After three days, all the sand had gone. By then, the balloons were floating over the United States and the bombs were dropped.

The balloon bombs were intended to start forest fires, set buildings on fire, cause thousands of casualties, and terrorize the civilian population. However, they failed. Only one of the 9,000 balloons proved to be fatal. When a young girl on a church outing in Oregon pulled one of the balloons down from a tree, the bomb it was carrying exploded, killing the girl and four friends, together with the woman who was looking after them. A few more balloons caused minor damage.

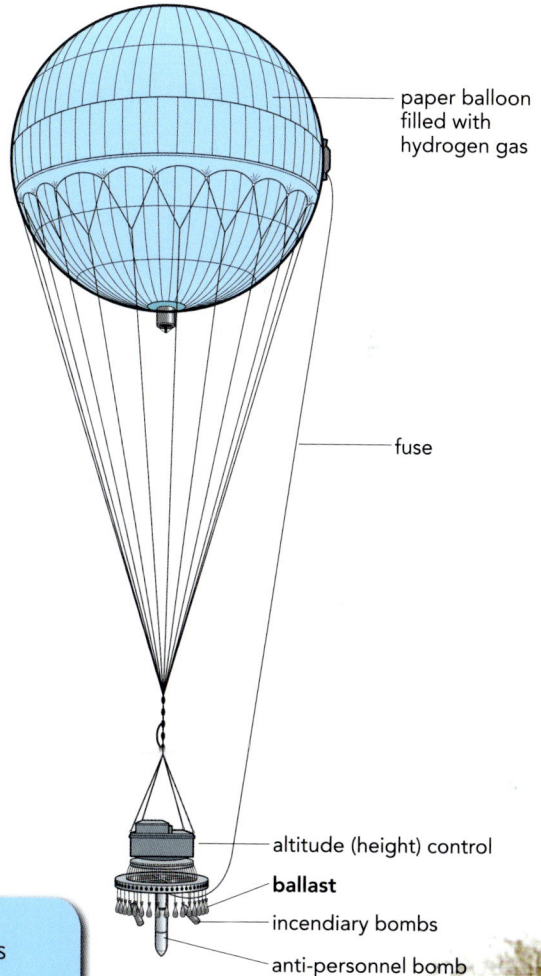

paper balloon filled with hydrogen gas

fuse

altitude (height) control

ballast

incendiary bombs

anti-personnel bomb

About 300 of the 9,000 balloons that were launched from Japan crossed the Pacific Ocean and were found in the United States.

No success

A serious shortcoming of the balloon attacks was that Japan had no way of measuring their effectiveness apart from picking up US news reports. However, US newspapers and radio stations agreed to a government request not to publish any information about the balloons while the war lasted. With no reports of successful attacks, Japan stopped sending the balloons.

What was learned?

Japan's balloon attack demonstrated the importance of controlling information in wartime. If the US public had known about the scale of the attacks, there could have been widespread panic. If the Japanese military forces had learned that hundreds of the bombs had reached the United States, they might have sent thousands more. A news black out prevented any panic and stopped further attacks.

Controlling information is equally important in military campaigns today. In 1990 Iraq invaded its neighbour, Kuwait. As multinational military forces gathered and prepared to push the Iraqi forces out of Kuwait, they ensured that Iraq had no access to satellite images of the area. This allowed them to keep their preparations secret and take the Iraqi forces by surprise.

Sand science

At first, nobody believed that the balloon bombs could possibly have flown all the way from Japan. **Geologists** finally proved where they had come from by analysing the sand in their sandbags. It didn't come from US or mid-Pacific beaches but from Japanese ones. The geologists were even able to pinpoint the actual beaches where the sand had been collected.

Ice ships   No.10

During World War II, the British government studied the possibility of building warships from ice. The work was known by the secret codename, Project Habakkuk.

Steel for building ships was in short supply in Britain during the war. As a result, there was a shortage of aircraft carriers. The carriers were needed to defend convoys of ships crossing the Atlantic Ocean, bringing vital supplies from North America to the United Kingdom. Planes from the carriers protected the convoys from attacks by U-boats (German submarines).

A British official, Geoffrey Pyke, had the idea of building aircraft carriers from ice instead of steel. He took the idea to his boss, Lord Louis Mountbatten, who was the Chief of Combined Operations. Part of Mountbatten's job was to produce new technology for the war. He asked scientists to come up with all sorts of ideas, no matter how crazy they seemed. The ice ship was exactly the sort of thing he was looking for. The British Prime Minister, Winston Churchill, was keen on it too. They thought the ships would be cheap and easy to make, so a large number of them could be built quickly.

This is an artist's impression of Project Habakkuk.

Strengthened ice

Ice ships would be unsinkable, because ice floats. They would also be quick and easy to repair – by pouring water into holes and freezing it. The ships could be up to 1,220 metres (4,000 feet) long and 180 metres (590 feet) wide. They would be more like floating airports than ships. Up to 150 aircraft would be stationed on each ice ship.

Experiments showed that ice on its own was too brittle. It split and shattered too easily, so scientists invented a new material from a mixture of wood pulp and water. When it was frozen, it was stronger than ice and it melted more slowly. They called the new material pykrete after Geoffrey Pyke. Pykrete could be moulded, cut, and drilled just like metal. Plans were made to build a fleet of pykrete ships. The final design was for ships that would be 610 metres (2,000 feet) long.

Testing the theory

First, a model was built to check whether the idea would actually work. It was built on Patricia Lake in Alberta, Canada. Slabs of ice and pykrete were laid inside a wooden frame. Cold air from freezer units was carried around the slabs through pipes to stop them from melting. They successfully stayed frozen all through the summer of 1943. A second experiment on Lake Louise showed that an ice ship's hull would have to be more than 10 metres (33 feet) thick to survive damage from bombs and torpedoes.

The Atlantic Gap

Until 1943 a large part of the middle of the Atlantic Ocean was beyond the range of land-based aircraft from the United Kingdom or North America. Here, U-boats could stalk convoys and pick off merchant ships without fear of being spotted or attacked from the air. It was called the Atlantic Gap or U-boat Alley. The ice ships were to be stationed here to protect shipping.

As the project went on, the researchers discovered problems. Ice looks solid, but it actually flows very slowly. A pykrete ship would gradually sag under its own weight unless it was kept at a temperature of −16 °C (3 °F). A bigger refrigeration plant would have to be built into the ship. The ice would also have to be reinforced with steel. As each problem was solved, the weight, size, and cost of the ships grew.

These men are working on a refrigeration system to keep the ice used for Project Habakkuk from melting.

Left to sink

In August 1943, Portugal gave the **Allies** permission to use runways on the Azores, a group of Atlantic islands. More aircraft carriers were also being built. There was no longer any need for the ice ships and so Project Habakkuk was dropped altogether. The floating structure on Patricia Lake was left to sink to the bottom of the lake, where the remains of it still lie today.

A Project Habakkuk ship would have been far bigger than any other World War II warship and even bigger than US Navy *Nimitz*-class aircraft carriers, the biggest warships in existence today.

	Project Habakkuk ship	USS *Yorktown* (WWII aircraft carrier)	USS *Nimitz* (modern supercarrier)
Length	610 metres (2,000 feet)	247 metres (809 feet)	333 metres (1,092 feet)
Displacement (amount of water shifted by the ship when floating)	1.8 million tonnes (2 million tons)	24,947 tonnes (27,500 tons)	87,300 tonnes (96,000 tons)

What was learned?

The main lesson learned from Project Habakkuk was that it is not as easy to build a ship from ice as it first seemed. An idea that looks promising can end up being impractical because of technical problems and cost. Countless military projects have, like Project Habakkuk, been cancelled due to rising costs and tricky problems. Sometimes, ideas that came to nothing are tried again later by someone else with more success, but nobody has tried to build a warship from ice since Project Habakkuk.

Flying wings

A flying wing is an aircraft whose structure is mostly wing. It does not have a body and tail. It is very efficient, because the whole aircraft produces lift. However, without a tail to steady it, a flying wing is also unstable and difficult to fly.

Several flying wing aircraft were built in the 1930s and 1940s. The US aircraft designer Jack Northrop had a special interest in flying wings. One of his projects was the Northrop XB-35, an experimental flying wing bomber.

Design work on the XB-35 began in 1942 and flight tests started in 1946. The tests were plagued with problems, but they showed that flying wing planes would fly. Northrop then built an improved version of the plane, called the YB-35. Like the XB-35, it was powered by **piston engines** and propellers. By the time the first YB-35 flew, in 1948, it was already out of date. By then, bombers and fighters were jet-powered. Two YB-35s were rebuilt with jet engines. They were called YB-49s. Both aircraft were destroyed in accidents and then the whole project was cancelled.

The Horten Brothers

Brothers Walter and Reimar Horten designed advanced aircraft in Germany in the 1940s, including flying wings. One of these was the Horten Ho-229, a flying wing fighter-bomber. After the war, a Ho-229 was sent to the United States for Northrop to study, because of his experience with flying wings.

FAIL!

A Northrop XB-35 flying wing bomber undergoes a test flight in 1946. At first, it seemed to be a success, but the plane developed a lot of mechanical problems.

What was learned?

The first flying wings worked, but they were too difficult and dangerous to fly. Northrop did eventually build a successful flying wing aircraft in the 1980s, the B-2 Spirit **stealth bomber**. By then, the development of computerized flight controls made it possible for pilots to handle flying wings safely.

Edwards Air Force Base

Edwards Air Force Base in California, USA is one of the world's most famous military and experimental aviation centres. Previously called the Muroc Army Air Field, it was renamed in memory of Captain Glen Edwards, the co-pilot of a YB-49 flying wing that crashed on 5 June 1948. The Forbes Air Force Base in Kansas was named after the plane's pilot, Major Daniel Forbes.

Northrop's flying wing designs of the 1940s led to the B-2 Spirit stealth bomber 40 years later. The B-2 has a wingspan of 52.4 metres (172 feet), exactly the same as that of the XB-35.

Superguns No.8

Superguns are the biggest and most powerful **artillery** weapons. After reading about the giant World War I Paris Gun, a young Canadian engineer called Gerald Bull was inspired to design big guns himself.

The Paris Gun

The Paris Gun was the biggest artillery gun of World War I. It was called the Paris Gun because it shelled Paris from a distance of 130 kilometres (80 miles). Its barrel was about 34 metres (111 feet) long.

A team of soldiers use a mobile crane to prepare the giant Paris Gun for firing during World War I.

In the early 1960s, Bull worked on a project that tested parts of new missiles by firing them high into the **atmosphere** from guns. Doing it this way was less expensive than launching them on rockets. It was called HARP (High Altitude Research Project). It used a gun made by welding two naval gun barrels together, end to end. The barrel was 36 metres (118 feet) long. It is still the longest working gun ever built. It fired **projectiles** higher and higher, eventually reaching a height of nearly 180 kilometres (111 miles). Bull claimed that the gun would be able to put a satellite in to orbit. However, in 1967 the Canadian government suddenly withdrew its funding for HARP.

Project Babylon

In 1988, Iraq agreed to pay for Bull's new supergun, now called Project Babylon. Its barrel would have been 156 metres (512 feet) long and 1 metre (3 feet) across. A small **prototype**, called Baby Babylon, was built and tested. Parts for Project Babylon were manufactured in several European countries. As it was illegal to sell arms to Iraq at that time, the manufacturers were told the parts were for the oil industry. However, weapons experts were suspicious, because the pipes were very thick and designed for huge pressures not found in oil pipelines. Some of the parts were seized before they reached Iraq, so the full-size Babylon supergun was never built.

By working for dangerous countries, such as Saddam Hussein's Iraq, Bull had made enemies. In March 1990, Gerald Bull was shot dead on his doorstep in Brussels, Belgium. His killer was never identified, but there are suspicions that Bull was killed by an agent acting for one of the countries most endangered by his weapons.

This Iraqi supergun was examined by a United Nations team in 1991.

Gas gun

Meanwhile, the US space agency NASA (National Aeronautics and Space Administration) was working on its own supergun to launch satellites. The project was called SHARP (Super High Altitude Research Project). Design work began in 1985 and it was ready for testing in 1992. It was a strange-looking gun. It had two barrels connected at one end. One barrel had a piston (a tight-fitting metal plug) at one end. The other end was sealed. An explosion sent the heavy piston hurtling down the barrel, squashing **hydrogen** gas inside the barrel. The pressure increased until the gas burst through the seal at the end and rushed into the second barrel. There, the sudden rush of high pressure gas fired a warhead out of the end of the barrel at almost nine times the speed of sound. The next step was to begin space-launching tests. However, the project was cancelled before this could be done, probably because the cost to achieve the first satellite launch was estimated at $1 billion.

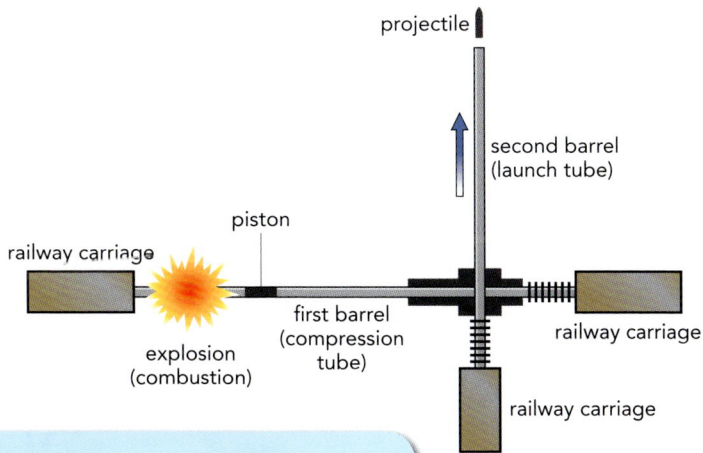

projectile

second barrel
(launch tube)

piston

railway carriage

first barrel
(compression
tube)

explosion
(combustion)

railway carriage

railway carriage

The SHARP gas gun generated recoil forces so great that the gun had to be anchored in place by several railway carriages weighing up to 91 tonnes (100 tons) each.

What was learned?

Superguns show that small objects can be fired up into the outer atmosphere, and more powerful superguns could probably fire satellites into space. Launching satellites from a supergun would be cheaper than using rockets, but rockets can launch much bigger and heavier satellites. Launching satellites by rocket is also a lot gentler than firing them out of a gun. Superguns used as military weapons are a bad idea too, because they are easy targets. In World War I it was hard to destroy the Paris Gun because it was so far from the front line. Today precise, **laser**-guided bombs would destroy a supergun on the first day of a war.

Newton's cannon

Gerald Bull was not the first person to think of firing objects into space from a gun. In 1728 the English scientist Isaac Newton wrote about a cannon he imagined being fired horizontally from a mountain-top. As the cannonball flew through the air, Earth's gravity would pull it down to the ground. If the gun could fire the cannonball faster, the ball would travel further before it hit the ground. If the cannonball went fast enough, it would never hit the ground.

Isaac Newton described how a cannonball fired fast enough would "fall" all the way around Earth. In other words, it would go into orbit.

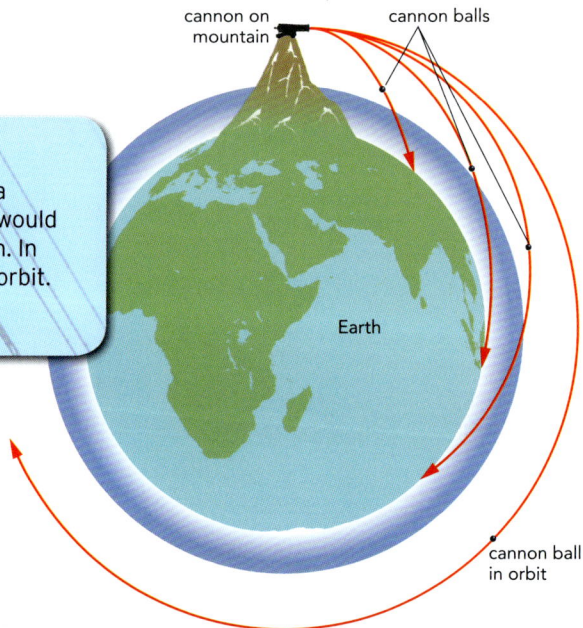

cannon on mountain

cannon balls

Earth

cannon ball in orbit

The Komet   No.7

During World War II, German engineers produced an extraordinary aircraft. It was a rocket-powered fighter called the Messerschmitt Me-163. It was the fastest fighter aircraft of the war.

Fast fighter

The Me-163, also known as the Komet, had a top speed of 960 kilometres (596 miles) per hour, compared to just over 700 kilometres (435 miles) per hour for the fastest **piston engine** fighter planes.

Komets would soar straight up through a group of bombers, firing at them on the way, and then dive down through them, firing again. The **Allies**' fighters couldn't catch a Komet. It zoomed past them at such a high speed that it was difficult to shoot down. So, why was it a failure?

Design flaws

The Komet only had enough fuel for 7.5 minutes of powered flight, or enough time for up to four bursts of fire at enemy aircraft. Then it became a glider.

The Komet's great speed was also a disadvantage. The Komet was so much faster than enemy planes that it flashed past them. The pilot had to aim and fire within a few seconds as well as fly the plane. The guns could not fire enough rounds to be effective in this short amount of time.

Komets served with the German air force between 1944 and 1945. During this time, they shot down only 9 aircraft of the Allies, while 14 Komets were shot down.

Test flights

Every new aircraft undergoes a series of test flights to study how it performs. The pilots who tested the Komet included Hanna Reitsch. She was one of the most experienced German test pilots. She was lucky to survive a terrible accident that happened when one test flight went wrong.

Reitsch had already tested an early version of the Komet, the Me-163a, and now prepared for her fifth test flight in the next version, the Me-163b. The first test flights didn't use rockets so that the engineers could find out how well the plane's shape suited flight on its own.

The plane was towed into the air by an Me-110 bomber. The Komet was such a small and simple aircraft that it did not have retractable wheels. Instead, it took off on a set of wheels that was dropped once the plane was airborne. This made the plane more streamlined so that it could fly smoothly at high speed. The Komet landed on a skid that ran along the bottom of the plane. Without wheels or suspension, landings could be very hard and some pilots suffered back injuries.

When Reitsch pulled the lever to drop the wheels, nothing happened. The wheels would not drop. The crew of the towing plane realized that Reitsch would need extra height to avoid crashing into the ground. They towed her up to 3,200 metres (10,500 feet). Then she cast off the tow-line and prepared to land.

Poisonous plane

Komets were dangerous to the pilots who flew them and the ground crews who refuelled them. The fuel was poisonous and much more explosive than normal aircraft fuel. The ground crews and pilots wore special clothing for protection. Fires and explosions were common. More Komets were destroyed in accidents than were shot down in combat.

The Messerschmitt Me-163 Komet was the first rocket-powered fighter. Nearly 400 Komets were produced in the 1940s.

FAIL!

FE500

Pilot food

The Komet's cockpit was unpressurized. The air pressure inside it was the same as the air pressure outside. So, when the plane climbed very quickly, the air pressure inside the cockpit fell quickly. Any gas trapped inside the pilot's stomach or intestines quickly expanded. Komet pilots had to eat a special low-fibre diet to keep "gas" to a minimum. Foods like baked beans were definitely not included!

Crash landing

The plane seemed to be flying well, but suddenly, just above the ground, it stalled. It lost lift because of the extra **drag** caused by the wheels. Reitsch said the plane "somersaulted over, lurched and sagged to a stop". She was badly injured but before she lost consciousness, she made a note of what had happened in case she didn't survive, then tied a handkerchief around her face so that her rescuers wouldn't be too shocked by her injuries.

What was learned?

The Komet showed that rocket-powered fighters were possible. However, military aircraft with one great advantage, such as speed in the case of the Komet, aren't always successful fighting machines. Designers have to look at the whole package and how it compares to enemy weapons. It also has to be practical to operate. More rocket-powered military aircraft were designed after World War II, but none of them went into production. The Komet is still the only rocket-powered fighter. After World War II, improvements in jet engines made rocket power unnecessary for aircraft, except for the fastest experimental planes. The X-1 and X-15 rocket planes went faster and higher than any previous planes.

WIN!

The Bell X-1 rocket plane made the first **supersonic** flight on 14 October 1947. Charles "Chuck" Yeager was at the controls.

The Strategic Defense Initiative

The **Strategic** Defense **Initiative** (SDI) was a military defence project announced by US President Ronald Reagan in 1983. Its aim was to defend the United States against a nuclear missile attack. It was a grand vision, to make the most destructive weapons ever invented a thing of the past. All the scientists and engineers had to do was to make it work.

US President Ronald Reagan launched the Strategic Defense Initiative with a speech on 23 March 1983. He said:

"I call upon the scientific community in our country, those who gave us nuclear weapons, to turn their great talents now to the cause of mankind and world peace, to give us the means of rendering those nuclear weapons **impotent** and **obsolete**."

The plan was for advanced **lasers** and other new weapons to shoot down nuclear missiles while they were high above the **atmosphere**. Some of these weapons would be on the ground and others would be orbiting Earth in space. The whole system would be under the control of a **supercomputer**. A lot of the technology necessary to make SDI work had not been developed yet.

Star Wars

SDI was such a futuristic project that it was nicknamed "Star Wars" after the science fiction films set in a galaxy far, far away. Estimates for what it might cost ranged from $100 billion to $1 trillion.

Space lasers

Some scientists thought SDI would never work, because it was so complex and needed new and untried technologies to work together with great precision. They were right. It proved to be too difficult to develop some of the weapons needed, especially the space lasers. Other people were against SDI, because it militarized space. Others said that even if it had worked, it would only defend against missiles that flew high above the atmosphere. It would be useless against nuclear attacks by **cruise missiles** and aircraft that could fly lower over the ground, and also nuclear bombs smuggled into the United States on board ships.

If SDI had worked, space lasers, like the one in this drawing, would destroy nuclear missiles as they soared away from their launchpads.

MIRACL

One part of the system that did work was a laser called MIRACL (**M**id-**I**nfra**r**ed **A**dvanced **C**hemical **L**aser). It was a hugely powerful laser – about 200 million times more powerful than the lasers used in CD players. MIRACL was designed to be used from the ground, not in space. Its job was to fire a high-power laser beam at enemy satellites to blind their cameras and burn out other sensors.

It was tested successfully in 1997, when its beam found and locked on to a US satellite coming to the end of its useful life. For the test, a very low-power beam was used, so the satellite was lit up but not destroyed.

The end of SDI

SDI was mainly designed to defend the United States against an attack that might involve many nuclear missiles launched from the **USSR**. When the USSR collapsed in 1991, the main enemy SDI was designed to deal with disappeared. This meant that there was not such a great need for SDI. It was finally abandoned by President Clinton in 1993 and replaced by defence systems that use missiles based on land and at sea.

A MAD policy

Nuclear-armed nations like the United States traditionally defend themselves by a policy called deterrence. They let it be known that any nuclear attack from another country will result in an immediate nuclear attack on that country. Any attacker knows that its own country is certain to be destroyed. It is a policy called Mutually Assured Destruction, or MAD.

Tests on the ground, such as this one, showed that a missile could be destroyed by the intense heat produced by a high-power laser beam.

What was learned?

When President Kennedy announced that the United States would land a man on the Moon by the end of the 1960s, the National Aeronautics and Space Administration (NASA) had to develop new spacecraft, rockets, and techniques to go to the Moon. They succeeded. However, just because a politician announces a project does not mean that it is technically possible. SDI was so complex, so expensive, and so far ahead of current technology that it could not be built.

Although the project was cancelled, the $30 billion spent on it did produce results. Some satellites now carry cameras that were developed for SDI. X-ray lasers used in scientific research were also developed for SDI. There will be more **spin-offs** from SDI for years to come as secret military research is declassified and civilian scientists are able to use it.

Bat bombs

One of the strangest ideas for attacking an enemy involved using armed bats! The bats weren't trained in any way. Instead, their natural habits were used to turn them into lethal weapons.

Pearl Harbor

On 7 December 1941, Japan carried out a surprise attack on the US naval base in Pearl Harbor, Hawaii. Fifteen warships were damaged or sunk, 188 aircraft were destroyed, and more than 2,000 military personnel and civilians were killed.

After the Japanese attack on Pearl Harbor during World War II, Dr Lytle Adams came up with the idea of the bat bomb. He suggested tying bombs to bats and dropping them from aircraft on to Japan. When the bats roosted in the roofs of houses, they would carry the bombs with them. The houses would then be set on fire when the bombs went off.

The President says yes

Dr Adams sent his proposal to the President on 12 January 1942. Many people were sending ideas to the government at this time. Most of the suggestions were impractical, but President Roosevelt approved the bat-bomb idea himself. Adams and his team visited 1,000 caves and 3,000 mines, searching for bats. The best bat for the job was the mastiff. It was the biggest bat in North America. It had a wingspan of 50 centimetres (20 inches) and could carry a 450-gram (16-ounce) stick of **dynamite** tied to its body. However, the team couldn't find the large numbers of mastiff bats they needed. In the end, they chose a tiny free-tailed bat. It weighed less than 10 grams (about ⅜ of an ounce), but it could carry a miniature bomb. The team found a colony of about 30 million free-tailed bats in Texas. They caught large numbers of the bats by holding a net across the entrance to their cave as they flew out.

Air drops

Scientists designed bombs light enough to be carried by the bats. While preparations for the first tests were made, the bats were kept in refrigerated containers to make them hibernate. The tests took place in May 1943. Thousands of bats were dropped from a B-25 bomber flying at a height of 1,500 metres (4,920 feet). The bats were dropped by parachute in cardboard boxes. The boxes opened at a height of 300 metres (984 feet) to let the bats fly out. The tests failed. The bats were still hibernating and simply fell to the ground. There were more tests, but the free-tailed bats refused to do what they were supposed to. Many of them avoided buildings and headed for freedom in the countryside.

The tests, which had been run by the US Army's Chemical Warfare Unit and the National Defense Research Committee (NDRC), came to a sudden stop when some of the armed bats escaped. Their bombs burned down an aircraft hangar where a general's car was parked!

Project X-Ray

In October 1943, the US Navy took over and renamed the project X-Ray. They put up enclosures on bat caves in Texas that trapped up to a million bats a night. However, before the end of the year the Navy handed the project over to the Marine Corps. They had some success: the bats started fires in buildings specially constructed for tests.

Free-tailed bats

Free-tailed bats get their name from their long mouse-like tail. They are among the fastest bats in the world. The bats eat moths that can damage crops, so they are a good form of pest control.

Full-scale bat drops from bombers were planned, but when senior officers learned that the bats would not be ready for a real attack until the middle of 1945, they cancelled the project.

FAIL!

This photograph shows a free-tailed bat, the kind used for bat bombs.

What was learned?

When armed live animals are released, they can't be controlled like machines. No matter how well-trained they are, they may go astray, perhaps putting the troops who released them in danger. This unpredictability, and public distaste at the use of animals as weapons, means that live animals with weapons are not used by conventional armed forces today. Armed robots and drones (remote-controlled pilotless planes) have taken the place of weaponized animals.

Anti-tank dogs

There have been other "weaponized" animals in the past, including cats, dolphins, and pigeons. During World War II, Britain used dead rats stuffed with explosives as booby-traps in Germany, and the **USSR** used anti-tank dogs. The dogs, carrying a pack full of explosives, were trained to run underneath any tanks they saw. They are said to have destroyed 300 German tanks.

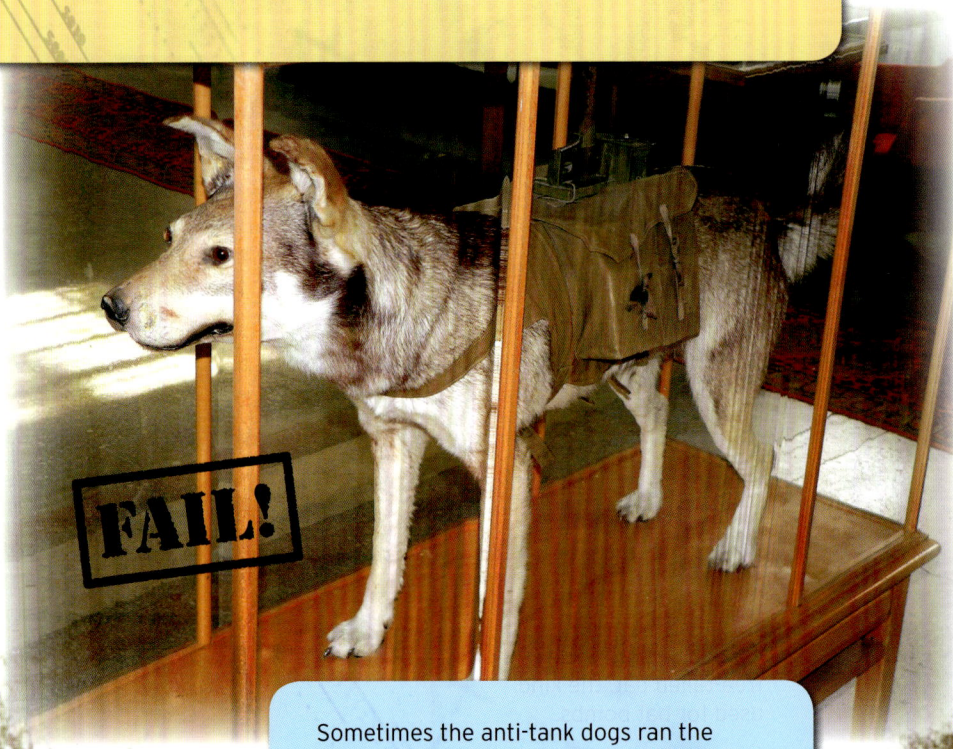

Sometimes the anti-tank dogs ran the wrong way and endangered **Soviet** troops. This stuffed anti-tank dog is in a museum.

Spy satellites

In the late 1990s, the US government started work on a new type of spy satellite. The project cost US taxpayers billions of dollars, but none of the satellites was built.

The company Boeing was chosen to build the satellites for the US National Reconnaissance Office, the government agency responsible for US spy satellites. The satellites were so advanced that some experts thought it would be impossible to build them within the project's budget. When engineers saw the design, they said it was so complex that it probably couldn't be built at all, but the development work continued.

Small and light

The new satellites were to be much smaller and lighter than previous spy satellites, which weighed more than a tonne and cost about $1 billion each. Smaller, lighter satellites could be launched in greater numbers and each satellite would cost less to launch.

There were problems with parts that didn't work properly, causing delays and increased costs. The government also asked for the design to be changed so that the satellites could do even more. The problems, delays, and design changes added billions of dollars to the cost. In 2005 a study found that another $5 billion would be needed, bringing the total cost to $18 billion, and the first satellite would be six years late. The project was cancelled.

Risky business

Spy satellites run the same risks as other satellites. They can be destroyed in launch accidents or they can break down in space. In August 1998 a billion dollar spy satellite was blown to pieces when its launch rocket exploded. In 2006 a spy satellite that was successfully placed in orbit became expensive space junk when its communications system failed.

What was learned?

A review of what went wrong found many problems. The project had been given to a manufacturer with no experience of building this type of satellite. The satellites were too complex. The budget (the amount of money provided for the project) was too small. Work on the project was not monitored closely enough. There were lots of lessons to learn for future projects.

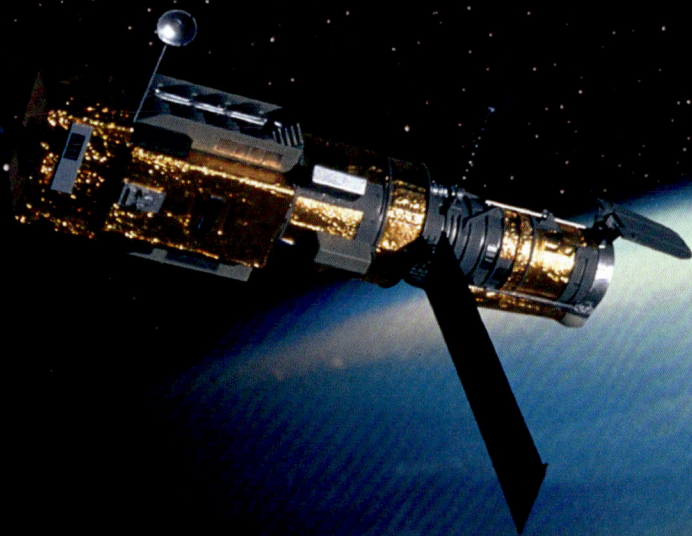

Spy satellites carry cameras to take pictures of the ground, and other instruments to collect a variety of information. Some of these satellites are the size of a bus.

The Great Panjandrum

The Great Panjandrum was a rocket-propelled wheel packed with explosives. It was designed to roll towards concrete barriers on beaches and blow a hole through them for troops landing from the sea.

The Great Panjandrum was built in the United Kingdom during World War II. It was made of two wheels separated by a drum in the middle. The drum contained more than a tonne of explosives. Each wheel was 3 metres (10 feet) across with rockets around its edge. When the rockets fired, the Panjandrum rolled along the ground. It was powerful enough to blow a hole in a concrete wall 3 metres (10 feet) high and more than 2 metres (6 feet) thick.

The Atlantic Wall

The Atlantic Wall was a line of defences built along the coast of Western Europe during World War II. It was built to stop troops landing on the coast from the sea. It was made of minefields, gun emplacements, concrete barriers, and barbed wire fences. It was the construction of the Atlantic Wall that led to the development of the Great Panjandrum.

The idea behind the Great Panjandrum was simple: it was a rocket-powered wheel. However, it was too difficult to get this simple idea to work in practice.

Steering the wheel

A **prototype** of the Great Panjandrum was built and tested on the beach at Westward Ho!, a seaside village in Devon, in September 1943. The drum was packed with sand instead of explosives. At first it seemed to be working, then some of the rockets on one side failed. The wheel on the other side turned faster and the Panjandrum started to go round in a circle. It was tested again with more rockets. It failed again. Another wheel was added, carrying even more rockets. The three-wheel Panjandrum failed too.

A new Panjandrum with more than 70 rockets was built. When it was tested, it turned around and headed back into the sea. Rockets flew off it in all directions. A steering system operated by cables pulled from a safe distance was tried. However, all the tests failed.

More modifications were made and a new prototype was tested in January 1944. This time, bumpy ground turned it off course and live rockets flew off in all directions again. Admirals and generals watching the test had to dive for cover. A cameraman recording the event was nearly run over when the Panjandrum headed straight for him. The project was scrapped soon afterwards.

What was learned?

Weapons that can't be steered accurately towards their target can be just as dangerous to friendly troops as they are to the enemy. Bullets, **artillery** shells, and some military rockets are not guided or steered, but they don't have to roll along on bumpy ground like the Great Panjandrum. With reliable rockets and a steering system that worked, the Great Panjandrum might have been an effective weapon, but with the technology of the 1940s, it was a failure.

This is an artist's impression of the Great Panjandrum.

What's in a name?

Panjandrum is a word invented in 1755 by the British actor and theatre manager, Samuel Foote. It appeared in his poem called "The Great Panjandrum". Charles Macklin, an actor, had claimed that he could memorize any text after reading it once. Samuel Foote wrote a nonsense poem to test Macklin, but there is no record of Macklin taking on the challenge. The weapon was named after it because of the poem's last lines:

"they all fell to playing the game of catch-as-catch-can, till the gunpowder ran out at the heels of their boots".

The *Vasa*

On 10 August 1628, thousands of people gathered on the Swedish coast at Stockholm to watch a great new warship put out to sea on its **maiden voyage**. The ship was called the *Vasa*. A few minutes later, it was at the bottom of the sea.

The *Vasa* was the world's mightiest warship. She was armed with 64 cannons on two gun decks, as well as a tall **aftercastle**. The Swedish king, Gustavus Adolphus, wanted the *Vasa* to set sail and join the Baltic Fleet as soon as possible, because Sweden was at war with Poland.

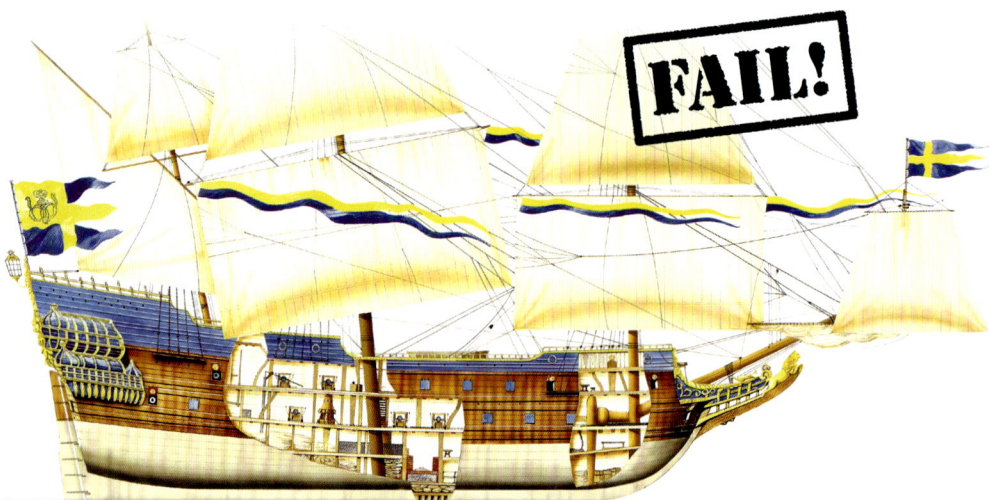

FAIL!

This cut-away drawing of the *Vasa* shows its decks and the **ballast** at the bottom.

Sunk

The *Vasa* set sail, and her cannons fired in salute. As the smoke cleared, people watching from the shore saw the great ship lean over in a gust of wind. She came back upright, but just for a few moments. A second, stronger, gust caught the ship and pushed her over further. Seawater poured in through the open **gun ports**. Horrified spectators watched the *Vasa* sink.

The king was furious. He demanded that whoever was responsible for the disaster should be punished. An inquiry was held and people were questioned. The inquiry discovered that the ship's stability had been tested, but the test had not gone well.

Thirty men had run back and forth across the deck to make the ship roll from side to side. The test had to be cut short, because the ship was rolling so much. In the end, the inquiry found that no single person was responsible for the disaster.

Ship design

In the 17th century, ship design advanced slowly by trial and error. Sometimes, the errors resulted in ships sinking. Warships were in greater danger of **capsizing** than merchant ships. Merchant ships carried cargo low down inside the hull, but warships had heavy cannons on top of the hull. The cannons could make a ship dangerously top-heavy.

This drawing shows the *Vasa* tipping and sinking as seawater floods the upper deck.

Mary Rose

The *Vasa* was not the first warship to overturn because it was top-heavy. Henry VIII's flagship, *Mary Rose*, met a similar fate 83 years earlier. In 1545, after more than 30 years' service, she set sail from the south coast of England. She had just been rebuilt, with an extra deck and bigger guns. As she turned to battle with French warships, she leaned over until her open gun ports were driven underwater. With thousands of people watching from the coast, the *Mary Rose* flooded and sank.

What was learned?

When the *Vasa* was **salvaged** in 1961, 120 tonnes (132 tons) of ballast was found in the bottom of her hull. Although this sounds like a lot, it was far too little ballast for the weight and size of the ship. Also, the gun ports on the upper gun deck were designed for **12-pounder** guns, but both decks were actually armed with heavier, **24-pounder** guns. The combination of too little ballast and too much weight above the **waterline** made the ship unstable. Added to this, the captain went to sea with the gun ports open. The second gust of wind that hit the ship was strong enough to roll her over, and water poured in through the open gun ports.

Later ship designers and builders learned how to build warships with up to four gun decks safely. They put the heaviest guns on the lowest deck and balanced the weight of the guns with extra ballast in the bottom of the hull.

The mighty *Vasa* sank when it was less than 2 kilometres (1.25 miles) into its first voyage.

FAIL!

The wreck of the *Vasa* was discovered in the 1950s and raised to the surface in 1961. She is now on display in Stockholm as the only surviving 17th-century ship to be salvaged almost intact.

Stable platform

The *Novgorod* and its sister-ship *Popov* were warships built for the Russian navy in the 1870s. The ships were as wide as they were long. In fact, they were circular! They were meant to be stable gun platforms that could sail into shallow water, but they were failures. They were slow and they pitched and rolled, even in quite calm sea. When one of the guns fired, the whole ship spun round!

The *Thresher*   No.1

The USS *Thresher* was one of the US Navy's nuclear-powered submarines. Her loss in an accident in 1963 changed the way US Navy submarines were built from then on.

The *Thresher* was a fast **attack submarine**. She was designed to hunt for **Soviet** submarines and chase them at up to 52 kilometres (32 miles) per hour underwater. Her nuclear-powered engines enabled her to stay submerged almost indefinitely.

The final dive

In April 1963, the *Thresher* began deep-diving exercises in the Atlantic Ocean east of Boston, Massachusetts. She was accompanied by the submarine rescue ship, USS *Skylark*, which was to monitor the exercises.

On 10 April, with the *Thresher* near her diving limit of almost 400 metres (1,312 feet), the *Skylark* received garbled messages from the submarine. The *Thresher* was in difficulty and trying to surface. Then the *Skylark* heard a dreadful sound, like air rushing into a tank. Nothing more was heard from the *Thresher*.

FAIL!

The USS *Thresher* was launched at the Portsmouth Naval Shipyard in the United States on 9 July 1960. She was named after a type of shark.

The **bathyscaphe** *Trieste*, which had dived to the deepest part of the world's oceans in 1960, later found the *Thresher* in pieces on the ocean floor at a depth of 2,600 metres (8,530 feet).

The loss of the *Thresher* was a great shock to everyone involved with submarines. She was the first US nuclear submarine to be lost at sea. An inquiry was held to find out what had happened.

USS *Squalus*

The USS *Squalus* was a submarine that sank in 1939. The *Squalus* was practising an emergency dive when seawater began flooding in. A ventilation valve had failed or been left open by mistake. The rear half of the submarine flooded, killing 26 sailors. A rescue chamber was lowered from a ship, the USS *Falcon*, and 33 survivors were brought to the surface. The *Squalus* was raised too. She was renamed *Sailfish* and returned to navy service.

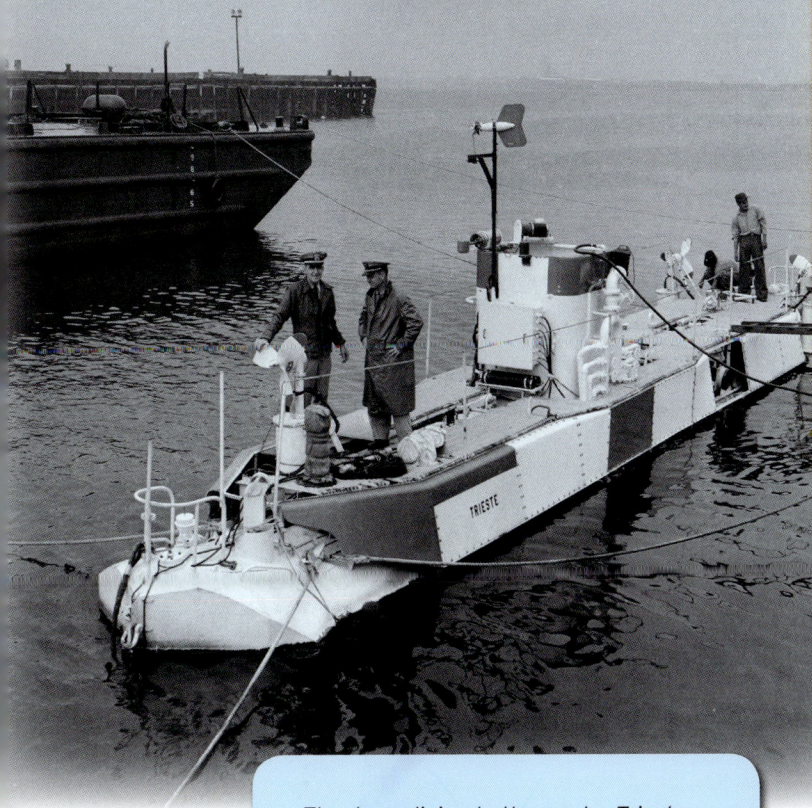

The deep-diving bathyscaphe *Trieste* prepares to take part in the search for the USS *Thresher*.

Faults and failures

The inquiry found that the *Thresher* probably sprang a leak somewhere in her seawater pipework. Water flooding into the submarine would have caused electrical faults and equipment failures. The **nuclear reactor** would have shut down automatically.

In an emergency, a submarine would normally be driven upwards by engine power. Then, the crew would force high-pressure air into the **ballast tanks** to push out the water. This would make the submarine lighter so that it floated to the surface. Without the nuclear reactor, the *Thresher* had no engine power, but why didn't the crew force air into the ballast tanks and float to the surface? They probably tried, but failed. Tests with the *Thresher's* sister vessel, the USS *Tinosa*, showed that the ballast tank pipework could become blocked with ice. This would have made it impossible for the crew to force air into the tanks. Without power and unable to control her depth, the *Thresher* would have sunk deeper and deeper until she reached about 600 metres (1,968 feet) and was crushed by the pressure of the water.

The *Scorpion* mystery

In May 1968 the submarine USS *Scorpion* vanished. Her last known position was about 80 kilometres (50 miles) south of the Azores, a group of islands in the Atlantic Ocean. Five months later, she was found in pieces at a depth of more than 3,000 metres (9,842 feet), south-west of the Azores.

The cause of the *Scorpion's* sinking was never discovered.

What was learned?

After the loss of the *Thresher*, the US Navy began a programme called SUBSAFE to make new submarines safer. Every part of a submarine that could fail and cause the loss of the vessel had to be made, fitted, tested, and repaired in strictly controlled ways. Since SUBSAFE began, no SUBSAFE-certified submarine has been lost.

The *Kursk*

On 12 August 2000, the Russian submarine *Kursk* sank in the Barents Sea. All 118 men on board died. It is thought that the **hydrogen** peroxide fuel in one of the submarine's torpedoes leaked and caused an explosion. This set off other torpedoes, which blew a hole in the submarine's hull. A British submarine, HMS *Sidon*, sank in 1955 for the same reason. As a result, Britain stopped using hydrogen peroxide as torpedo fuel. The governments and military forces of different nations have differing ideas about what is safe and what is an unacceptable risk.

The massive Russian submarine *Kursk* sank after an explosion caused by a faulty torpedo.

Timeline

1045   The first known use of solid fuel rockets, by Chinese military forces. These were the same type of rockets that would be used about 900 years later to build the Great Panjandrum.

1545   The British warship *Mary Rose* sinks when water floods in through her **gun ports**

1628   The Swedish warship *Vasa* sinks because poor design resulted in her being unstable

1776   The *Turtle* submarine attacks HMS *Eagle* unsuccessfully

1783   The first manned flight in a **hydrogen** balloon is made by Jacques Charles and Nicolas Robert. This type of balloon would be used to carry bombs from Japan to the United States during World War II.

1873   The circular warship *Novgorod* is launched. The bigger *Popov* is launched two years later.

1897   The first modern submarine, the *Holland VI*, is launched. It becomes the USS *Holland*, the US Navy's first submarine.

1918   The Paris Gun, the biggest **artillery** gun of World War I, is built. Stories of this gun later inspire a Canadian engineer, Gerald Bull, to build a new generation of superguns.

1920s   **Acoustic** mirrors are built along the coast of England to detect the sound of approaching enemy aircraft

1930s   **Radar** replaces acoustic mirrors. Early warning stations equipped with this new technology are built around the coast of England.

1941   The Messerschmitt Me-262, the world's first jet fighter, makes its first flight

1943   The US Army and Navy conduct tests of bat bombs that they hope to drop over Japan. The tests are a failure and the project is cancelled.

1943   Work begins on Project Habakkuk, research aimed at
        building ships from ice

1944   The Great Panjandrum rocket-powered explosive wheel
        is scrapped when it fails to work

1944   Japan attacks the United States with bombs carried across
        the Pacific Ocean by hydrogen balloons

1946   The Northrop XB-35 flying wing bomber makes its first flight

1954   The USS *Nautilus*, the world's first nuclear-powered
        submarine, is launched

1955   The British submarine, HMS *Sidon*, sinks because of an
        explosion in its hydrogen peroxide torpedo fuel. This leads
        to an end of the use of hydrogen peroxide torpedo fuel in
        British submarines.

1957   The **USSR** launches the first satellite, *Sputnik 1*

1959   The experimental North American Aviation X-15
        rocket-plane makes its first flight

1960   The USS *Thresher* submarine is launched

1963   The USS *Thresher* sinks, leading to the SUBSAFE system for
        making submarines safer

1983   US President Ronald Reagan announces the **Strategic
        Defense Initiative**

1990   Parts for a supergun called Project Babylon are seized in
        Europe. The gun was being constructed for Iraq.

1993   The US government abandons the Strategic Defense Initiative
        (SDI) when the project proves to be too complex and costly
        to develop

2000   The Russian submarine *Kursk* sinks because of an explosion in
        its hydrogen peroxide torpedo fuel

2005   A US spy satellite project is scrapped when it proves too difficult
        and costly to build

Glossary

12-pounder cannon that fires a cannonball weighing 12 pounds (5.5 kilograms)

24-pounder cannon that fires a cannonball weighing 24 pounds (11 kilograms)

acoustic to do with sound

aftercastle tall structure built on top of the back of a warship, used by soldiers to fire down on to the decks of other ships

Allies countries (the United Kingdom, United States, USSR, and others) that fought the Axis powers (Germany, Italy, Japan, and others) during World War II

artillery large, heavy cannons or guns

atmosphere air around Earth, or, generally, the gas around any planet or moon

attack submarine fast submarine whose job is to hunt and attack other submarines and surface ships

ballast weight added to a submarine to make it dive; something heavy, such as lead or rocks, placed in the bottom of a ship to make it stable

ballast tank compartment in a submarine that can be filled with water to make a submarine heavier so that it dives

bathyscaphe manned diving craft consisting of a crew compartment suspended by a float

capsize turn upside down

Confederate of the Confederate states, the southern states that left the United States in 1861, sparking the American Civil War, which lasted until 1865

conning tower platform on top of a submarine, where an officer can stand and "con" (command) the vessel. The conning tower is inside a submarine's sail, the tall fin-like structure on top of a submarine.

cruise missile guided missile with wings

drag resistance to movement. Drag is a force that pushes against a plane, or any other object that moves through air.

dynamite type of explosive material

fuse device that sets off an explosion

geologist scientist who studies the structure of Earth and the rocks it is made of

gun port square hole cut in the side of a ship for a gun to fire through

hydrogen lightest of all gases. A balloon filled with hydrogen rises in the air. Hydrogen is also flammable and can be used as fuel.

impotent without strength

infrared type of ray similar to light, but which is invisible to the human eye and carries heat away from where it is made

initiative fresh approach

laser device that produces a beam of intense, pure light of only one colour

maiden voyage first journey made by a ship or submarine after its sea trials

mortar short, light artillery gun for firing shells high in the air over short distances

nuclear reactor device that gives out large amounts of energy in the form of heat by means of nuclear reactions in its fuel

obsolete no longer useful

piston engine engine that works like a car engine

projectile object hurled or fired through the air, such as a bullet, artillery shell, or missile

prototype first example of something new, such as the first of a new type of aircraft or weapon

radar Radio Detection and Ranging, an electronic system for detecting ships and aircraft by bouncing radio waves off them and receiving the reflections. Radar also shows the direction and speed of ships and aircraft.

salvage rescue the remains of a ship from the sea

Soviet of the Soviet Union, another name for the USSR

spin-off technology or a process developed for one purpose that then proves to be useful elsewhere. Advanced clothing textiles, lubricants, batteries, cameras, paint, and even cordless vacuum cleaners are spin-offs from space research.

stealth bomber military aircraft designed to be very difficult to detect by radar

strategic concerned with planning aimed at achieving a long-term aim

supercomputer one of the fastest computers in the world

supersonic faster than the speed of sound, which varies from about 1,060 kilometres (659 miles) per hour to 1,225 kilometres (761 miles) per hour depending on the temperature of the air

Union of the federal government of the United States, which fought the Confederate Army in the American Civil War (1861–1865)

USSR Union of Soviet Socialist Republics, also known as the Soviet Union. The communist state that existed from 1922 to 1991, including Russia and 14 other republics.

waterline level of water on the hull of a floating boat or ship

Find out more

Books: non-fiction

Attack Fighters, Ian Graham (Heinemann Library, 2008)

Destroy After Reading: the World of Secret Codes, Mary Colson (Raintree, 2011)

Military Vehicles, Ian Graham (Heinemann Library, 2008)

Why Things Don't Work: Tank, David West (Raintree, 2007)

Books: fiction

From the Earth to the Moon, Jules Verne (Dover Publications, 2009)

20,000 Leagues Under the Sea, by Jules Verne and Pauline Francis (Evans Brothers, 2004)

Websites

www.royalnavalmuseum.org/info_sheets_Habbakkuk.htm
The Royal Naval Museum website describes Project Habbakkuk.

www.vasamuseet.se/en
There is a lot of information about the famous Swedish warship *Vasa* at the *Vasa* Museum website.

www.maryrose.org
Henry VIII's warship, *Mary Rose*, its sinking, and its recovery are described on this website.

Further research

If you enjoyed reading about the planes, submarines, guns, warships, satellites, and other military and government projects that failed or were cancelled, you might also enjoy finding out more about these projects that suffered a similar fate:

- The Sikorsky X-Wing aircraft
- The TSR2 supersonic bomber
- The XB-70 Valkyrie supersonic bomber
- The Ryan X-13 Vertijet
- Lockheed XFV and Convair XFY Pogo "tail-sitter" planes
- The Convair NB-36 and Tupolev Tu-95LAL nuclear-powered bombers
- The Saunders-Roe SR.177 jet/rocket powered fighter
- The Rockwell X-30 spaceplane
- The Panzerjäger Tiger Elefant tank destroyer
- The Stridsvagn 103, or S-tank

Index